Goodbye Long Hair

Written By: Elsie Guerrero

ISBN: 978-1-7327573-8-7

Goodbye Long Hair

Copyright © 2019 Elsie Guerrero

ELSIE PUBLISHING CO.
WWW.ELSIEGUERRERO.COM

Elsie Publishing Co.
Washington, DC
www.elsieguerrero.com
202.670.3282

Printed in the United States of America.

This book is dedicated to my friend, Karina Perla, and to all the children who have been diagnosed with cancer. My prayers are with you.

Gaby es una niña hermosa con cabello largo y castaño. Su cabello es tan largo que pasa sus rodillas. Gaby ama su largo cabello castaño con todo su carazón.

Gaby is a beautiful girl with long brown hair. Her hair is so long that it passes her knees. Gaby absolutely loves her long brown hair.

Gaby y su madre fueron al hospital para un chequeo anual. El doctor entró y se sorprendió al verle el cabello. Le preguntó, "¿Alguna vez has pensado donar tu cabello?"

Gaby, confundida, dijo, "¿Por qué donaría mi cabello? Amo mi cabello largo." "Tenemos muchos niños en el hospital que necesitan cabello," dijo el doctor. Gaby no podía entender por qué el doctor le pediría su cabello. Ella ama su cabello.

Gaby and her mother went to the hospital for Gaby's annual checkup. The doctor walked in and was amazed by Gaby's hair. He asked, "Have you ever thought about donating your hair?"

Gaby, confused, said, "Why would I donate my hair? I love my long hair."

"We have a lot of children in the hospital who need hair," said the doctor. But, Gaby still could not understand why the doctor would ask for her hair. She loves her hair.

Gaby, el doctor y su madre fueron a caminar por el hospital y luego entraron a una habitación. El doctor le presento Jenny a Gaby, una paciente con leucemia.

———◆◆◆———

Gaby, the doctor and her mother went for a walk around the hospital and then walked into a patient's room. The doctor introduced Gaby to Jenny, a leukemia cancer patient.

Los ojos de Gaby se abrieron completamente, sorprendida. Dijo "¡Dios mío! ¡No tienes cabello! ¿Dónde está tu cabello?"

—◆◆—

Gaby's eyes got wide. "OMG"! You do not have hair! Where is your hair?" asked Gaby.

Jenny se sintió incómoda, y bajo su cabeza. Estaba muy consciente de que no tenía cabello. Gaby no tenía intención de herir sus sentimientos, pero nunca había visto a una niña sin cabello. Gaby ama su cabello.

———✦———

Jenny felt so awkward that she put her head down. Gaby did not mean to hurt her feelings, but she had never seen a girl with no hair. Gaby loves her hair.

Cuando Gaby llegó a casa, comenzó a bailar y a decirse a sí misma, "Realmente amo mi cabello largo." Su madre la escuchó y dijo, "Sé que lo haces cariño, pero deberías pensar en los niños como Jenny que no tienen cabello."

———

When Gaby got home she started dancing and saying to herself, "I really love my long hair." Her mother overheard Gaby and said, "I know you do honey, but you should think about children like Jenny who do not have hair."

El día siguiente, Gaby le preguntó a su madre si podían visitar a Jenny porque quería aprender más sobre la leucemia. La madre de Gaby la miró sorprendida de que quisiera volver al hospital.

—⋘⋙—

The next day, Gaby asked her mother if they could visit Jenny because she wanted to learn more about leukemia cancer. Gaby's mother looked at her, surprised that she wanted to go back to the hospital.

Gaby entró a la habitación de Jenny con un gran oso de peluche y globos. Gaby estaba tan emocionada de ver a Jenny, pero cuando llegó, Jenny no se veía bien. Jenny no se sentía bien.

Gaby walked into Jenny's room with a big bear and balloons. Gaby was so excited to see Jenny, but when she arrived, Jenny did not look good. Jenny was not feeling well.

"¿Qué pasa, Jenny?" preguntó Gaby.

"Tuve quimioterapia hoy y ahora no me siento bien", respondió Jenny. La quimioterapia es el tratamiento del cáncer con citotóxicos y otras drogas para quitar el cáncer.

———◦◦———

"What is wrong Jenny?" asked Gaby.

"I had chemotherapy today and now I feel tired and weak," Jenny responded. Chemotherapy is used to treat cancer by using cytotoxic and other drugs to remove the cancer.

Gaby le preguntó a Jenny "¿Cómo te sentirías si tuvieras cabello largo?"

Jenny respondió, "¡No me importa qué tan largo sea mi cabello mientras tenga cabello! Me encantaría tener cabello."

———◆◆———

Gaby asked Jenny, "How would you feel if you had long hair?"

Jenny responded, "I would not care how long my hair was as long as I had hair!"

De noche, mientras Gaby se preparaba para la cama, miró su cabello y se dijo a ella misma, "¡Amo mi cabello largo, pero Jenny necesita cabello!"

Gaby contempló donar su cabello.

At night, while Gaby was in bed, she looked at her hair and said to herself, "I love my long hair, but Jenny needs hair!"

Gaby contemplated donating her hair.

El día siguiente, Gaby fue al hospital a decirle a Jenny la buena noticia de que había decidido cortar su cabello, pero Jenny estaba muy enferma para recibir visita. Jenny no podía hablar, caminar, o abrir sus ojos. Los doctores tuvieron que vigilarla todo el día.

———◈◈———

The next day, when Gaby went to the hospital to tell Jenny the good news that she decided to donate her hair, Jenny was too sick to have visitors. Jenny was unable to talk, walk, or open her eyes. The doctors had to watch her all day.

Gaby estaba triste al no poder ver a Jenny y no entendía por qué esto le estaba pasando.

Gaby was sad she could not see her and did not understand why this was happening to Jenny.

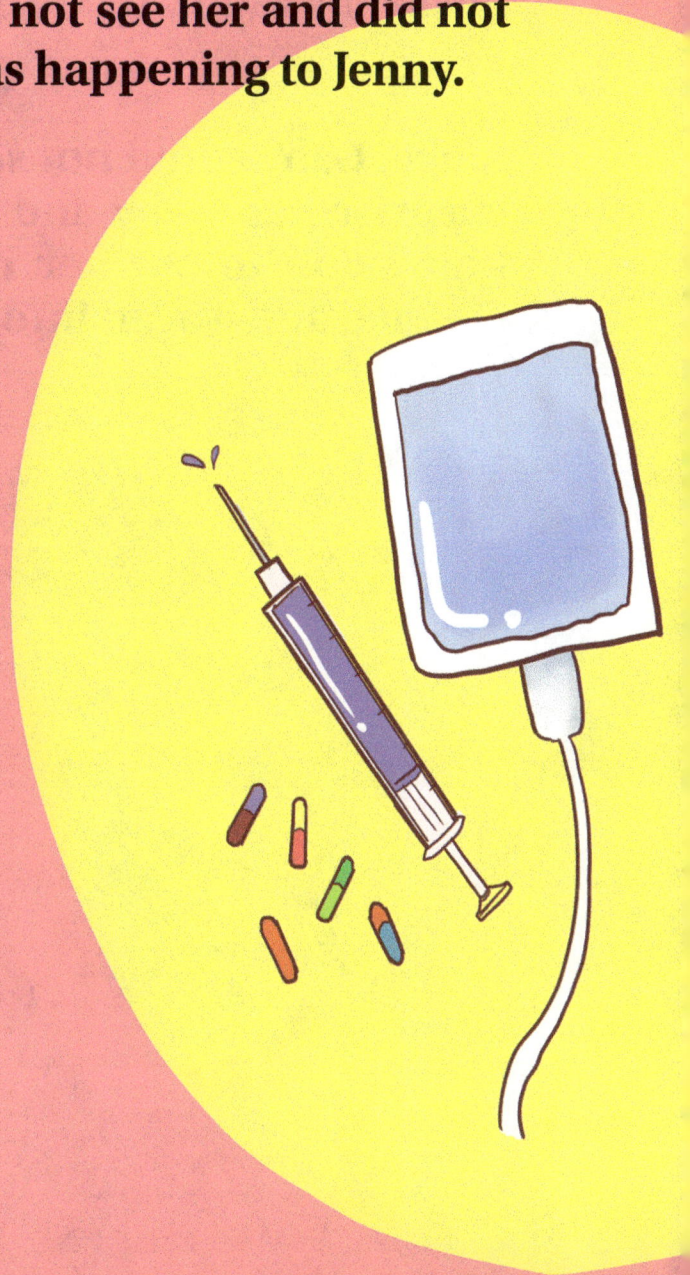

Ya que Gaby no podía ver a Jenny, ella decidió sorprenderla. Gaby y su madre fueron a la peluquería a cortar su cabello. Gaby estaba emocionada. No podía esperar. El cabello fue luego limpiado y tejido en una peluca especial.

Since, Gaby could not see Jenny, she decided to surprise her. Gaby and her mother went to the hair salon to cut her hair. The hair was then cleaned and woven into a special wig.

Gaby estaba emocionada. No podía esperar para sorprender a Jenny. Al día siguiente, Gaby fue a ver a Jenny y la sorprendió con la hermosa peluca de largo cabello castaño. Jenny estaba emocionada de probarlo. Le dio un gran abrazo a Gaby y dijo "¡Muchas gracias!"

❦

Gaby was excited. She could not wait to surprise Jenny. The next day, Gaby went to see Jenny and surprise her with the beautiful wig with long brown hair. Jenny was excited to try it on. She gave Gaby a big hug and said, "Thank you so much!"

Gaby ahora tiene el cabello corto y Jenny tiene cabello.

———◦◦———

Gaby now has short hair and Jenny has hair.

**Thank you Karina and Gaby,
Perla for sharing your story!**

www.ingramcontent.com/pod-product-compliance
Lightning Source LLC
Chambersburg PA
CBHW050635150426

42811CB00052B/836